Affiliate Marketing Without a Website: A Simple Guide to Making Money Online

Roy Hendershot

Published by Roy Hendershot, 2024.

AFFILIATE MARKETING WITHOUT A WEBSITE: A SIMPLE GUIDE TO MAKING MONEY ONLINE

First edition. June 8, 2024.

Written by Roy Hendershot.

Table of Contents

Introduction: The Basics of Affiliate Marketing

How affiliate marketing works is quite simple. You join an affiliate program, choose products to promote, and get a unique link to track your sales. When someone clicks on your link and makes a purchase, you earn a commission. It's a win-win situation. The seller gets more sales, and you earn money for your efforts.

One of the biggest benefits of affiliate marketing is that you don't need to create your own products. This means you can focus on marketing and promoting, which can be much easier and quicker than developing your own product from scratch. Additionally, you can work from anywhere with an internet connection, making it a flexible option for many people.

There are some common misconceptions about affiliate marketing that need to be addressed. Some people think it's a get-rich-quick scheme, but that's not true. It takes time and effort to build a successful affiliate marketing business. Others believe you need a website to succeed, but there are many other ways to promote affiliate products without one.

Why don't you need a website? There are many platforms available where you can promote affiliate products. Social media, email marketing, and online communities are just a few examples. These platforms can be just as effective, if not more so, than a traditional website.

Setting realistic expectations is crucial in affiliate marketing. While it's possible to make a lot of money, it won't happen overnight. You need to be patient, consistent, and willing to learn. It's important to understand that success will come with time and effort.

The affiliate marketing ecosystem consists of several key players. The advertiser or merchant is the one who creates the product. The affiliate, which would be you, promotes the product. Then, there are consumers who buy the product. Finally, there are affiliate networks that act as intermediaries between the affiliates and the merchants.

As an affiliate marketer, your role is to connect the right audience with the right product. This involves understanding your audience's needs and finding products that solve their problems. You'll need to be persuasive and credible to succeed.

There are different types of affiliate programs available. Some pay per sale, others pay per click, and some even pay per lead. It's important to choose a program that aligns with your goals and interests. This will make it easier to promote the products genuinely and effectively.

Choosing the right niche is crucial. A niche is a specific area of interest or expertise. By focusing on a niche, you can target a specific audience and become an authority in that area. This can make it easier to build trust and credibility with your audience.

Trust and transparency are vital in affiliate marketing. If your audience trusts you, they are more likely to follow your recommendations. Be honest about your affiliations and only promote products you believe in. This will help you build a loyal following over time.

Building your personal brand is another important aspect. Your brand is how people perceive you. It's important to present yourself as knowledgeable, trustworthy, and approachable. This can help you attract and retain a loyal audience.

Identifying your target audience is essential. You need to understand who you are trying to reach and what their needs are. This will help you create content that resonates with them and promotes products they are interested in.

Understanding the buyer's journey is also crucial. This is the process that consumers go through before making a purchase. It includes awareness, consideration, and decision stages. By understanding this process, you can create content that guides your audience through each stage.

Social proof is a powerful tool in affiliate marketing. This can include testimonials, reviews, and case studies. People are more likely to buy a product if they see that others have had a positive experience with it. Use social proof to build trust and credibility with your audience.

The growth of the affiliate marketing industry has been significant over the years. More and more companies are using affiliate programs to increase their sales. This means there are more opportunities for you as an affiliate marketer.

Key metrics to track include clicks, conversions, and earnings. These metrics will help you understand how well your marketing efforts are performing. Use this data to make informed decisions and improve your strategies.

There are many tools and resources available to help you succeed in affiliate marketing. These can include keyword research tools, analytics platforms, and content creation tools. Utilize these resources to streamline your efforts and improve your results.

The legal side of affiliate marketing is important to understand. This includes disclosures and compliance with advertising regulations. Make sure you are transparent about your affiliations and follow the rules to avoid any legal issues.

Staying updated with industry trends is crucial. The affiliate marketing landscape is constantly evolving. Keep learning and adapting to stay ahead of the competition. Follow industry blogs, attend webinars, and join affiliate marketing communities to stay informed.

Time management is key to success. With so many tasks to handle, it's important to stay organized and prioritize your efforts. Use tools like calendars and to-do lists to keep track of your tasks and stay on top of your game.

Consistency is essential. Posting regularly and engaging with your audience consistently will help you build a loyal following. This applies to all your marketing efforts, from social media posts to email newsletters.

Setting your goals is the first step towards success. Define what you want to achieve and create a plan to get there. Break down your goals into smaller, manageable tasks and track your progress along the way.

Creating an action plan will help you stay focused and motivated. Outline the steps you need to take to achieve your goals and set deadlines for each task. This will help you stay on track and make steady progress.

As you prepare for your affiliate marketing journey, remember that success won't come overnight. Be patient, stay consistent, and keep learning. With time and effort, you can build a successful affiliate marketing business without a website.

Chapter 1: Leveraging Social Media Platforms

———

Social media platforms have become powerful tools for affiliate marketers. They allow you to reach a large audience and engage with them directly. Each platform has its own unique features and benefits, so it's important to choose the right one for your niche.

Creating a compelling profile is the first step. Your profile is often the first impression people will have of you. Make sure it reflects your brand and includes important information about what you do and what you offer.

Building a strong following takes time and effort. Engage with your audience regularly by posting valuable content, responding to comments, and participating in conversations. The more active and engaged you are, the more followers you will attract.

Content creation is key to social media success. Share a mix of content, including articles, videos, infographics, and personal updates. This will keep your audience interested and engaged. Make sure your content is relevant to your niche and provides value to your followers.

Engaging with your audience is crucial. Respond to comments and messages promptly, and participate in conversations. This will help you build relationships with your followers and increase their trust in you.

Using hashtags effectively can increase the visibility of your posts. Research popular hashtags in your niche and use them in your posts. This will help you reach a wider audience and attract more followers.

Live videos are a powerful tool for engagement. They allow you to interact with your audience in real-time and build a stronger connection with them. Use live videos to share valuable content, answer questions, and provide updates.

Collaborating with influencers can help you reach a larger audience. Find influencers in your niche and build relationships with them. Collaborate on content, run joint promotions, and leverage each other's audiences.

Running social media contests can increase engagement and attract new followers. Offer prizes that are relevant to your niche and encourage your followers to participate. This will help you build excitement and increase your reach.

Stories and reels are popular features on many social media platforms. Use them to share behind-the-scenes content, updates, and promotions. They are a great way to keep your audience engaged and interested.

Paid advertising options are available on most social media platforms. These can help you reach a larger audience and drive more traffic to your affiliate links. Experiment with different ad formats and targeting options to find what works best for you.

Analyzing social media metrics is crucial for success. Track your engagement, reach, and conversions to understand how well your efforts are performing. Use this data to make informed decisions and improve your strategies.

There are many case studies of successful social media marketers that you can learn from. Study their strategies, see what works for them, and apply similar tactics to your own efforts. This can help you achieve better results.

Avoid common mistakes like being too promotional or not engaging with your audience. Focus on providing value and building relationships. This will help you build a loyal following and increase your success.

Each social media platform has its own best practices. Learn what works best for each platform and tailor your strategies accordingly. This will help you maximize your reach and engagement.

Staying consistent with posting is important. Create a content calendar and schedule your posts in advance. This will help you stay organized and ensure you are consistently engaging with your audience.

Responding to comments and messages is crucial for building relationships. Make sure you are active and responsive. This will show your audience that you care about them and value their input.

Building a community around your brand can increase loyalty and engagement. Encourage your followers to participate in discussions, share their experiences, and connect with each other. This will help you create a supportive and engaged community.

Leveraging user-generated content can increase trust and credibility. Encourage your followers to share their experiences and tag you in their posts. Share their content on your own profile to show appreciation and build a sense of community.

Creating shareable content can increase your reach. Share content that is informative, entertaining, and valuable. This will encourage your followers to share it with their own networks, increasing your visibility.

Understanding platform algorithms is crucial for success. Each platform has its own algorithm that determines which posts are shown to users. Learn how these algorithms work and tailor your content to increase your chances of being seen.

The role of visual content is important. Posts with images or videos tend to perform better than text-only posts. Make sure your visual content is high-quality and relevant to your niche.

Staying updated with social media trends is important. Social media is constantly evolving, and staying current with trends can help you stay ahead of the competition. Follow industry blogs, attend webinars, and participate in social media communities to stay informed.

Monetizing your social media presence can be done in various ways. You can use affiliate links, sponsored posts, or sell your own products. Experiment with different monetization strategies to find what works best for you.

Chapter 2: Utilizing Email Marketing

Email marketing is a powerful tool for affiliate marketers. It allows you to build a direct relationship with your audience and promote your affiliate products effectively. Despite the rise of social media, email marketing remains one of the most effective marketing channels.

Building your email list is the first step. Offer something valuable in exchange for people's email addresses, such as a free ebook, a discount, or access to exclusive content. This will encourage people to subscribe to your list.

Creating effective lead magnets is crucial. A lead magnet is something you offer for free in exchange for someone's email address. Make sure it is relevant to your niche and provides value to your audience.

Crafting irresistible opt-in forms is important for converting visitors into subscribers. Your opt-in form should be simple, attractive, and clearly communicate the benefits of subscribing. Use persuasive language and highlight the value you are offering.

Understanding email marketing platforms is essential. There are many platforms available, each with its own features and benefits. Choose a platform that meets your needs and budget. Some popular options include Mailchimp, ConvertKit, and AWeber.

Segmenting your audience can increase the effectiveness of your email campaigns. By dividing your subscribers into smaller groups based on their interests and behaviors, you can send more targeted and relevant emails. This can lead to higher engagement and conversions.

Writing engaging email copy is crucial. Your emails should be clear, concise, and provide value to your subscribers. Use a friendly tone and personalize your messages to make them more relatable and engaging.

Designing eye-catching email templates can make your emails stand out. Use a clean and professional design that reflects your brand. Include images, buttons, and other visual elements to make your emails more attractive and easy to read.

Personalizing your emails can increase engagement. Use your subscribers' names and include personalized recommendations based on their interests and behaviors. This can make your emails feel more relevant and valuable.

Automating your email campaigns can save you time and effort. Set up automated sequences to welcome new subscribers, follow up on purchases, and re-engage inactive subscribers. This can help you stay connected with your audience and drive more sales.

Analyzing email metrics is crucial for success. Track your open rates, click-through rates, and conversions to understand how well your campaigns are performing. Use this data to make informed decisions and improve your strategies.

Avoiding the spam folder is important. Make sure your emails comply with spam regulations and follow best practices to avoid being marked as spam. This can help you maintain a good sender reputation and ensure your emails reach your subscribers' inboxes.

Best practices for email subject lines include keeping them short, clear, and engaging. Use action-oriented language and create a sense of urgency to encourage opens. Test different subject lines to see what works best for your audience.

Timing your emails for maximum impact can increase engagement. Experiment with different send times and days to find the optimal time for your audience. This can help you reach your subscribers when they are most likely to engage with your emails.

Providing value to your subscribers is crucial for building trust and loyalty. Share valuable content, tips, and resources that are relevant to your niche. This can help you build a strong relationship with your audience and increase their willingness to follow your recommendations.

The role of follow-up emails is important. Follow up with subscribers who haven't opened your emails or taken the desired action. This can help you re-engage them and increase your chances of driving conversions.

Case studies of successful email campaigns can provide valuable insights. Study what worked for others and apply similar tactics to your own campaigns. This can help you achieve better results and avoid common mistakes.

Common mistakes to avoid include being too promotional, not segmenting your audience, and neglecting to analyze your metrics. Focus on providing value, personalizing your emails, and continually improving your strategies.

Strategies for re-engaging inactive subscribers include sending re-engagement emails, offering special promotions, and asking for feedback. This can help you bring back subscribers who have lost interest and increase your overall engagement.

Legal considerations for email marketing include complying with regulations like the CAN-SPAM Act and GDPR. Make sure you include a clear unsubscribe link in your emails and obtain proper consent from your subscribers.

Integrating email with other marketing channels can increase your overall effectiveness. Use email to promote your social media profiles, blog posts, and other content. This can help you reach your audience through multiple touchpoints and increase your visibility.

The importance of A/B testing cannot be overstated. Test different elements of your emails, such as subject lines, copy, and design, to see what works best. Use the results to optimize your campaigns and achieve better results.

Staying updated with email marketing trends is crucial. The email marketing landscape is constantly evolving, and staying current with trends can help you stay ahead of the competition. Follow industry blogs, attend webinars, and participate in email marketing communities to stay informed.

Building long-term relationships with subscribers is essential for success. Focus on providing consistent value, engaging with your audience, and building trust.

This can help you create a loyal following and increase your long-term success in affiliate marketing.

Chapter 3: Influencer Marketing

Influencer marketing involves partnering with influencers to promote your affiliate products. Influencers are individuals who have a large following and can influence the purchasing decisions of their audience. By leveraging their influence, you can reach a larger audience and increase your sales.

The benefits of working with influencers are numerous. They can help you reach a larger and more targeted audience, increase your credibility, and drive more sales. Influencers can also create high-quality content that showcases your products in a positive light.

Identifying the right influencers is crucial for success. Look for influencers who have a large and engaged following in your niche. Check their engagement rates, the quality of their content, and their overall reputation. This will help you find influencers who can effectively promote your products.

Building relationships with influencers takes time and effort. Start by engaging with their content, leaving thoughtful comments, and sharing their posts. Once you've established a connection, reach out to them with a personalized message and propose a collaboration.

Negotiating collaborations is an important step. Discuss the terms of the collaboration, including the type of content, the compensation, and the expectations. Make sure both parties are clear on the details and agree on the terms.

Creating mutually beneficial partnerships is key. Ensure that the collaboration provides value to both you and the influencer. This will help you build a long-term relationship and increase the chances of successful collaborations in the future.

Influencer marketing platforms can help you find and connect with influencers. These platforms provide tools for searching, managing, and tracking influencer collaborations. Some popular options include AspireIQ, Traackr, and Influencity.

Crafting effective campaigns involves setting clear goals, creating engaging content, and tracking your results. Work closely with the influencer to ensure the content aligns with your brand and resonates with their audience.

Measuring campaign success is crucial. Track key metrics like reach, engagement, and conversions to understand how well your campaigns are performing. Use this data to make informed decisions and improve your future collaborations.

Case studies of successful influencer campaigns can provide valuable insights. Study what worked for others and apply similar tactics to your own campaigns. This can help you achieve better results and avoid common mistakes.

Avoiding common pitfalls is important. Some common mistakes include partnering with the wrong influencers, not setting clear expectations, and not tracking your results. Focus on building strong relationships, setting clear goals, and continually improving your strategies.

Legal and ethical considerations are crucial in influencer marketing. Ensure that your collaborations comply with advertising regulations and disclose any affiliations. This will help you maintain transparency and trust with your audience.

Leveraging micro-influencers can be effective. Micro-influencers have smaller but highly engaged followings. They can be more affordable and provide more authentic recommendations. Consider partnering with micro-influencers to reach a more targeted audience.

Influencer takeovers are a fun and engaging way to promote your products. Allow an influencer to take over your social media account for a day and share their experience with your products. This can increase engagement and provide fresh content for your audience.

Utilizing affiliate links with influencers can increase your sales. Provide influencers with unique affiliate links to track their sales and reward them for their efforts. This can motivate them to promote your products more effectively.

14

Content co-creation strategies involve working with influencers to create content together. This can include blog posts, videos, and social media posts. Co-created content can provide a fresh perspective and increase engagement.

The role of authenticity is important in influencer marketing. Ensure that your collaborations feel genuine and authentic. Influencers should promote products they genuinely like and believe in. This will help build trust with their audience.

Budgeting for influencer marketing is crucial. Determine how much you can afford to spend on influencer collaborations and allocate your budget accordingly. Consider both monetary compensation and other forms of value, such as free products or exclusive access.

Influencer marketing for different niches requires different strategies. Tailor your approach to the specific needs and preferences of your niche. This will help you create more effective and relevant campaigns.

Integrating influencer marketing with other strategies can increase your overall effectiveness. Use influencer collaborations to complement your social media, email, and content marketing efforts. This can help you reach your audience through multiple touchpoints.

Trends in influencer marketing are constantly evolving. Stay updated with the latest trends and adapt your strategies accordingly. Follow industry blogs, attend webinars, and participate in influencer marketing communities to stay informed.

Building long-term relationships with influencers is crucial. Focus on providing value, maintaining open communication, and being respectful of their time and efforts. This will help you build strong, lasting partnerships.

The power of testimonials and reviews cannot be overstated. Encourage influencers to share their honest opinions and experiences with your products. This can increase trust and credibility with their audience.

Utilizing influencer marketing tools can streamline your efforts. These tools can help you find influencers, manage collaborations, and track your results. Some popular options include Hootsuite, BuzzSumo, and Klear.

The future of influencer marketing looks promising. As the industry continues to grow, new opportunities and trends will emerge. Stay adaptable and open to new strategies to stay ahead of the competition.

Chapter 4: Creating High-Quality Content

Creating high-quality content is essential for affiliate marketing success. Quality content can attract and engage your audience, build trust, and drive conversions. It's important to focus on providing value and meeting the needs of your audience.

Understanding your audience's needs is the first step. Conduct research to learn about their interests, problems, and preferences. This will help you create content that resonates with them and provides solutions to their problems.

Researching your topics is crucial for creating informative and valuable content. Use reliable sources and gather as much information as possible. This will help you provide accurate and comprehensive content that adds value to your audience.

Writing engaging blog posts is an effective way to share valuable information and promote your affiliate products. Focus on providing useful tips, insights, and solutions. Use a friendly tone and make your posts easy to read and understand.

Creating informative videos can increase engagement and reach a wider audience. Videos are a popular content format and can effectively showcase your products. Make sure your videos are high-quality and provide valuable information.

Designing eye-catching infographics can make complex information more digestible. Infographics are visually appealing and can easily convey key points. Use them to present data, explain processes, and highlight important information.

Recording podcasts is another effective way to share valuable content. Podcasts are convenient for your audience to consume and can cover a wide range of topics. Make sure your podcasts are well-produced and provide valuable insights.

Repurposing content for different platforms can increase your reach. Turn blog posts into videos, infographics, or social media posts. This will help you reach different audiences and maximize the value of your content.

Content calendars and planning are essential for staying organized and consistent. Plan your content in advance and schedule your posts. This will help you maintain a regular posting schedule and keep your audience engaged.

The role of SEO in content marketing is important. Use relevant keywords, optimize your titles and descriptions, and create high-quality content. This will help you improve your search engine rankings and attract more organic traffic.

Utilizing keywords effectively can increase your visibility. Conduct keyword research to find relevant and high-traffic keywords. Use them naturally in your content to improve your search engine rankings.

Writing for readability is crucial. Use simple language, short sentences, and clear headings. This will make your content easy to read and understand. Break up large blocks of text with images, bullet points, and subheadings.

The power of storytelling can make your content more engaging and memorable. Share personal anecdotes, case studies, and success stories. This will help you connect with your audience on an emotional level.

Case studies of successful content strategies can provide valuable insights. Study what worked for others and apply similar tactics to your own content. This can help you achieve better results and avoid common mistakes.

Avoiding common content mistakes is important. Some common mistakes include being too promotional, not providing value, and neglecting to optimize for SEO. Focus on creating valuable, informative, and engaging content.

Leveraging user-generated content can increase trust and credibility. Encourage your audience to share their experiences and contribute content. Share their content on your own platforms to show appreciation and build a sense of community.

Engaging with your audience through content is crucial. Respond to comments, ask questions, and encourage discussions. This will help you build relationships and increase engagement.

Analyzing content performance is important for improving your strategies. Track key metrics like views, engagement, and conversions. Use this data to understand what works and make informed decisions.

Staying consistent with content creation is essential. Create a content calendar and stick to a regular posting schedule. This will help you maintain a steady flow of content and keep your audience engaged.

The role of visual content is important. Posts with images or videos tend to perform better than text-only posts. Make sure your visual content is high-quality and relevant to your niche.

Creating shareable content can increase your reach. Share content that is informative, entertaining, and valuable. This will encourage your audience to share it with their own networks, increasing your visibility.

Integrating content with affiliate links can increase your sales. Include relevant affiliate links in your content naturally and provide context. This will help you promote your products without being too promotional.

The importance of originality cannot be overstated. Create unique and original content that stands out. This will help you differentiate yourself from the competition and attract more attention.

Tools for content creation can streamline your efforts. Use tools like Canva for designing visuals, Grammarly for checking grammar, and Google Analytics for tracking performance. These tools can help you create high-quality content more efficiently.

Trends in content marketing are constantly evolving. Stay updated with the latest trends and adapt your strategies accordingly. Follow industry blogs, attend webinars, and participate in content marketing communities to stay informed.

Chapter 5: Leveraging Video Marketing

Video marketing has become increasingly popular and effective. Videos can capture attention, convey information quickly, and engage your audience. Leveraging video marketing can help you reach a wider audience and drive more sales.

Choosing the right video platforms is the first step. YouTube, Facebook, Instagram, and TikTok are popular options. Each platform has its own unique features and benefits. Choose the platforms that are most relevant to your niche and audience.

Creating engaging video content is crucial. Focus on providing value, entertaining your audience, and addressing their needs. Use high-quality visuals and clear audio to make your videos more appealing.

The power of live streaming cannot be overstated. Live videos allow you to interact with your audience in real-time, answer questions, and provide updates. This can help you build a stronger connection with your audience.

Utilizing YouTube for affiliate marketing can be highly effective. Create a YouTube channel, upload regular content, and optimize your videos for search. Include affiliate links in your video descriptions and encourage viewers to check them out.

Optimizing video titles and descriptions can increase your visibility. Use relevant keywords, create catchy titles, and write detailed descriptions. This will help your videos rank higher in search results and attract more viewers.

Engaging with your audience through videos is crucial. Respond to comments, ask questions, and encourage discussions. This will help you build relationships and increase engagement.

Case studies of successful video marketers can provide valuable insights. Study what worked for others and apply similar tactics to your own videos. This can help you achieve better results and avoid common mistakes.

The role of thumbnails is important. Thumbnails are the first thing viewers see and can influence their decision to watch your video. Create eye-catching thumbnails that accurately represent your video content.

Video editing basics are essential for creating high-quality videos. Use editing software to trim, add effects, and enhance your videos. Make sure your videos are polished and professional.

Using analytics to improve videos is crucial. Track key metrics like views, watch time, and engagement. Use this data to understand what works and make informed decisions.

Collaborating with other creators can increase your reach. Partner with other YouTubers or social media influencers to create content together. This can help you reach new audiences and build relationships with other creators.

Monetizing your video content can be done in various ways. Use affiliate links, sponsored content, or ads to generate revenue. Experiment with different monetization strategies to find what works best for you.

Video marketing best practices include creating valuable content, optimizing for search, and engaging with your audience. Focus on providing value, being consistent, and continually improving your strategies.

Common mistakes to avoid include being too promotional, neglecting SEO, and not engaging with your audience. Focus on creating valuable and engaging content, optimizing for search, and building relationships with your viewers.

Integrating affiliate links in videos can increase your sales. Include relevant links in your video descriptions and provide context. This will help you promote your products without being too promotional.

The importance of call to actions cannot be overstated. Encourage viewers to take the desired action, whether it's subscribing to your channel, checking out your affiliate links, or sharing your videos. Clear and compelling call to actions can increase engagement and conversions.

Utilizing social media for video promotion can increase your reach. Share your videos on your social media profiles, join relevant groups, and engage with your audience. This can help you attract more viewers and drive more traffic to your videos.

Understanding different video formats is important. Each platform has its own preferred formats and requirements. Make sure your videos meet these requirements and are optimized for each platform.

The role of scriptwriting is crucial for creating engaging videos. Plan your content in advance and write a script to guide your videos. This will help you stay organized and ensure your videos are clear and concise.

Staying consistent with video uploads is essential. Create a content calendar and stick to a regular posting schedule. This will help you maintain a steady flow of content and keep your audience engaged.

Building a YouTube channel can increase your reach and credibility. Optimize your channel with relevant keywords, create eye-catching channel art, and upload regular content. This will help you attract more subscribers and build a loyal following.

Leveraging trends and challenges can increase your visibility. Participate in popular trends and challenges in your niche. This can help you attract more viewers and stay relevant.

Tools for video creation can streamline your efforts. Use tools like Adobe Premiere Pro for editing, Canva for designing thumbnails, and TubeBuddy for optimizing your videos. These tools can help you create high-quality videos more efficiently.

The future of video marketing looks promising. As video continues to grow in popularity, new opportunities and trends will emerge. Stay adaptable and open to new strategies to stay ahead of the competition.

Chapter 6: Participating in Online Forums and Communities

———

Online forums and communities are valuable platforms for affiliate marketers. They allow you to engage with a targeted audience, share valuable information, and promote your affiliate products. Participating in these communities can help you build relationships and increase your reach.

Identifying relevant online communities is the first step. Look for forums and communities that are active and focused on your niche. This will help you connect with people who are interested in your products and services.

Building credibility and trust is crucial in online communities. Provide valuable information, answer questions, and engage in meaningful discussions. This will help you establish yourself as an authority and build trust with the community members.

Engaging with community members is important. Respond to questions, participate in discussions, and share your knowledge. This will help you build relationships and increase your visibility in the community.

Sharing valuable content can increase your credibility and attract more attention. Share articles, videos, and other content that provides value to the community. Make sure your content is relevant and helpful.

Utilizing signature links can promote your affiliate products. Most forums allow you to include a signature at the end of your posts. Include your affiliate links in your signature to drive traffic and generate sales.

Participating in Q&A sessions can showcase your expertise. Answer questions related to your niche and provide helpful information. This will help you build credibility and attract more attention to your affiliate products.

Case studies of successful community engagement can provide valuable insights. Study what worked for others and apply similar tactics to your own efforts. This can help you achieve better results and avoid common mistakes.

Avoiding spammy behavior is important. Focus on providing value and building relationships. Avoid excessive self-promotion and follow the community guidelines. This will help you maintain a positive reputation and build trust with the community members.

The role of moderators is important. Moderators ensure that the community guidelines are followed and maintain a positive environment. Engage with the moderators and follow their guidelines to ensure a smooth experience.

Creating your own community can increase your reach and control. Start a forum or online group focused on your niche. This will allow you to engage with your audience more directly and build a loyal following.

Leveraging Reddit for affiliate marketing can be effective. Reddit is a popular platform with many niche communities. Participate in relevant subreddits, share valuable content, and engage with the community members.

Utilizing niche forums can increase your reach. Look for forums that are focused on specific topics related to your niche. This will help you connect with a more targeted audience and increase your chances of success.

Building relationships with influencers in online communities can increase your reach. Engage with influencers, share their content, and collaborate on projects. This can help you reach a larger audience and build credibility.

The importance of consistency cannot be overstated. Engage with the community regularly and provide valuable content. This will help you build relationships and maintain your visibility.

Best practices for forum engagement include being respectful, providing value, and following the community guidelines. Focus on building relationships and providing helpful information. This will help you build credibility and trust.

Common mistakes to avoid include being too promotional, neglecting to engage with the community, and not following the guidelines. Focus on providing value, building relationships, and maintaining a positive reputation.

Integrating affiliate links in forum posts can increase your sales. Include relevant links in your posts naturally and provide context. This will help you promote your products without being too promotional.

Staying updated with community trends is important. Online communities are constantly evolving, and staying current with trends can help you stay ahead of the competition. Follow industry blogs, attend webinars, and participate in online community discussions to stay informed.

Engaging in meaningful discussions can increase your credibility and attract more attention. Share your knowledge, ask questions, and provide valuable insights. This will help you build relationships and increase your visibility.

The role of social proof is important. Share testimonials, reviews, and case studies to build trust and credibility. This will help you attract more attention and increase your chances of success.

Providing value to the community is crucial. Share valuable content, answer questions, and engage in meaningful discussions. This will help you build relationships and increase your credibility.

Building your personal brand is important. Establish yourself as an authority in your niche and build trust with the community members. This will help you attract more attention and increase your chances of success.

Using analytics to track engagement can help you improve your strategies. Track key metrics like post views, engagement, and conversions. Use this data to understand what works and make informed decisions.

Leveraging community feedback can provide valuable insights. Ask for feedback, listen to the community members, and make improvements based on their suggestions. This will help you build a stronger relationship with the community.

Future of online communities looks promising. As more people engage in online communities, new opportunities and trends will emerge. Stay adaptable and open to new strategies to stay ahead of the competition.

Chapter 7: Utilizing Paid Advertising

———

Paid advertising can be a powerful tool for affiliate marketers. It allows you to reach a larger audience, drive more traffic, and generate more sales. Utilizing paid advertising effectively can help you achieve your marketing goals.

The basics of paid advertising include understanding different ad formats, targeting options, and budgeting. Each platform has its own unique features and benefits. Choose the platforms that are most relevant to your niche and audience.

Choosing the right advertising platforms is crucial. Google Ads, Facebook Ads, Instagram Ads, and LinkedIn Ads are popular options. Each platform has its own unique features and benefits. Choose the platforms that are most relevant to your niche and audience.

Setting a budget is important for managing your advertising costs. Determine how much you can afford to spend on ads and allocate your budget accordingly. Monitor your spending and adjust your budget as needed to achieve your goals.

Crafting compelling ad copy can increase your click-through rates. Use clear, concise, and persuasive language to encourage people to click on your ads. Highlight the benefits of your products and include a clear call to action.

Designing eye-catching ad creatives can make your ads stand out. Use high-quality images, videos, and graphics to capture attention. Make sure your ad creatives are relevant to your niche and visually appealing.

Targeting the right audience is crucial for success. Use the targeting options available on each platform to reach your ideal audience. This can include demographic targeting, interest targeting, and behavior targeting.

Utilizing retargeting strategies can increase your conversions. Retargeting allows you to show ads to people who have previously visited your website or engaged with your content. This can help you re-engage potential customers and drive more sales.

Analyzing ad performance is important for improving your strategies. Track key metrics like clicks, impressions, and conversions. Use this data to understand how well your ads are performing and make informed decisions.

Case studies of successful ad campaigns can provide valuable insights. Study what worked for others and apply similar tactics to your own campaigns. This can help you achieve better results and avoid common mistakes.

Avoiding common advertising mistakes is important. Some common mistakes include targeting the wrong audience, not testing different ad creatives, and not analyzing your results. Focus on creating relevant and engaging ads, testing different strategies, and continually improving your campaigns.

Best practices for different platforms can increase your effectiveness. Each platform has its own best practices for creating and optimizing ads. Learn what works best for each platform and tailor your strategies accordingly.

The role of A/B testing is crucial for optimizing your ads. Test different ad elements, such as headlines, images, and calls to action, to see what works best. Use the results to optimize your ads and achieve better results.

Integrating paid ads with affiliate marketing can increase your sales. Use ads to drive traffic to your affiliate links and landing pages. This can help you reach a larger audience and generate more sales.

Utilizing PPC campaigns can be effective for driving traffic. Pay-per-click (PPC) campaigns allow you to pay only when someone clicks on your ad. This can be a cost-effective way to drive targeted traffic to your affiliate links.

Understanding ad metrics is important for measuring success. Track key metrics like click-through rates, conversion rates, and return on ad spend. Use this data to understand how well your ads are performing and make informed decisions.

Leveraging social media ads can increase your reach. Use Facebook Ads, Instagram Ads, and LinkedIn Ads to promote your affiliate products. These platforms offer powerful targeting options and can help you reach a larger audience.

The importance of landing pages cannot be overstated. A landing page is the page people land on after clicking your ad. Make sure your landing pages are optimized for conversions and provide a seamless user experience.

Creating effective call to actions can increase your click-through rates. Use clear and compelling language to encourage people to take the desired action. This can include clicking your ad, visiting your website, or making a purchase.

Budgeting for ad campaigns is crucial for managing your costs. Determine how much you can afford to spend on ads and allocate your budget accordingly. Monitor your spending and adjust your budget as needed to achieve your goals.

The role of analytics is important for measuring success. Track key metrics like clicks, impressions, and conversions. Use this data to understand how well your ads are performing and make informed decisions.

Staying updated with advertising trends is crucial. The advertising landscape is constantly evolving, and staying current with trends can help you stay ahead of the competition. Follow industry blogs, attend webinars, and participate in advertising communities to stay informed.

Building long-term advertising strategies can increase your success. Focus on creating sustainable and scalable ad campaigns. This will help you achieve consistent results and grow your affiliate marketing business over time.

Legal considerations for advertising are important. Ensure that your ads comply with advertising regulations and guidelines. This will help you avoid legal issues and maintain a positive reputation.

Tools for ad creation and management can streamline your efforts. Use tools like Google Ads, Facebook Ads Manager, and Canva for designing and managing your ads. These tools can help you create high-quality ads more efficiently.

Future of paid advertising looks promising. As more businesses invest in paid advertising, new opportunities and trends will emerge. Stay adaptable and open to new strategies to stay ahead of the competition.

Chapter 8: Creating a YouTube Channel

———

Creating a YouTube channel can be a powerful tool for affiliate marketing. YouTube is one of the largest and most popular video platforms, and it offers a great opportunity to reach a large audience and promote your affiliate products.

The power of YouTube for affiliate marketing cannot be overstated. YouTube allows you to create engaging video content, build a loyal following, and drive traffic to your affiliate links. By creating valuable and entertaining videos, you can attract a large audience and generate more sales.

Setting up your YouTube channel is the first step. Create a Google account if you don't already have one, and then use it to create your YouTube channel. Choose a name that reflects your brand and niche, and customize your channel with a profile picture, banner, and description.

Creating engaging video content is crucial for success. Focus on providing value, entertaining your audience, and addressing their needs. Use high-quality visuals and clear audio to make your videos more appealing. Plan your content in advance and create a content calendar to stay organized and consistent.

Optimizing video titles and descriptions can increase your visibility. Use relevant keywords, create catchy titles, and write detailed descriptions. This will help your videos rank higher in search results and attract more viewers. Include your affiliate links in the video descriptions and encourage viewers to check them out.

Utilizing YouTube SEO can increase your search rankings. Use relevant keywords in your titles, descriptions, and tags. Create high-quality thumbnails that attract clicks. This will help your videos rank higher in search results and attract more views.

Engaging with your audience through videos is crucial. Respond to comments, ask questions, and encourage discussions. This will help you build relationships and increase engagement. Create a community around your channel and foster a sense of belonging.

Case studies of successful YouTube channels can provide valuable insights. Study what worked for others and apply similar tactics to your own channel. This can help you achieve better results and avoid common mistakes.

The role of thumbnails is important. Thumbnails are the first thing viewers see and can influence their decision to watch your video. Create eye-catching thumbnails that accurately represent your video content. Use high-quality images and clear text to make your thumbnails more appealing.

Video editing basics are essential for creating high-quality videos. Use editing software to trim, add effects, and enhance your videos. Make sure your videos are polished and professional. Experiment with different editing styles to find what works best for your audience.

Using analytics to improve videos is crucial. Track key metrics like views, watch time, and engagement. Use this data to understand what works and make informed decisions. Analyze your audience demographics and behavior to tailor your content accordingly.

Collaborating with other creators can increase your reach. Partner with other YouTubers or social media influencers to create content together. This can help you reach new audiences and build relationships with other creators. Collaborate on projects, cross-promote each other's channels, and share each other's content.

Monetizing your YouTube channel can be done in various ways. Use affiliate links, sponsored content, or ads to generate revenue. Experiment with different monetization strategies to find what works best for you. Apply for the YouTube Partner Program to earn money from ads.

Video marketing best practices include creating valuable content, optimizing for search, and engaging with your audience. Focus on providing value, being consistent, and continually improving your strategies. Experiment with different content formats, such as tutorials, reviews, and vlogs.

Common mistakes to avoid include being too promotional, neglecting SEO, and not engaging with your audience. Focus on creating valuable and engaging content, optimizing for search, and building relationships with your viewers. Avoid clickbait titles and misleading thumbnails.

Integrating affiliate links in videos can increase your sales. Include relevant links in your video descriptions and provide context. This will help you promote your products without being too promotional. Encourage viewers to check out your links and provide honest reviews and recommendations.

The importance of call to actions cannot be overstated. Encourage viewers to take the desired action, whether it's subscribing to your channel, checking out your affiliate links, or sharing your videos. Clear and compelling call to actions can increase engagement and conversions.

Utilizing social media for video promotion can increase your reach. Share your videos on your social media profiles, join relevant groups, and engage with your audience. This can help you attract more viewers and drive more traffic to your videos. Use relevant hashtags and tags to increase visibility.

Understanding different video formats is important. Each platform has its own preferred formats and requirements. Make sure your videos meet these requirements and are optimized for each platform. Experiment with different formats to see what works best for your audience.

The role of scriptwriting is crucial for creating engaging videos. Plan your content in advance and write a script to guide your videos. This will help you stay organized and ensure your videos are clear and concise. Use a friendly and conversational tone to make your videos more relatable.

Staying consistent with video uploads is essential. Create a content calendar and stick to a regular posting schedule. This will help you maintain a steady flow of content and keep your audience engaged. Plan your content in advance and batch-produce videos to stay ahead.

Building a YouTube channel can increase your reach and credibility. Optimize your channel with relevant keywords, create eye-catching channel art, and upload regular content. This will help you attract more subscribers and build a loyal following. Engage with your audience and foster a sense of community.

Leveraging trends and challenges can increase your visibility. Participate in popular trends and challenges in your niche. This can help you attract more viewers and stay relevant. Stay updated with the latest trends and adapt your content accordingly.

Tools for video creation can streamline your efforts. Use tools like Adobe Premiere Pro for editing, Canva for designing thumbnails, and TubeBuddy for optimizing your videos. These tools can help you create high-quality videos more efficiently. Experiment with different tools to find what works best for you.

The future of video marketing looks promising. As video continues to grow in popularity, new opportunities and trends will emerge. Stay adaptable and open to new strategies to stay ahead of the competition. Keep learning and experimenting with new content formats and techniques.

Chapter 9: Using Pinterest for Affiliate Marketing

———

Pinterest is a visual search engine that can be a powerful tool for affiliate marketing. It allows you to create and share visually appealing content, attract a targeted audience, and drive traffic to your affiliate links. Using Pinterest effectively can help you achieve your marketing goals.

The basics of Pinterest include creating and optimizing your profile, creating engaging pins, and organizing your boards. Choose a profile picture that reflects your brand, write a clear and concise bio, and include relevant keywords. This will help you attract more followers and increase your visibility.

Creating a business account on Pinterest is important for accessing analytics and advertising features. A business account allows you to see how your pins are performing, track your audience demographics, and run ads. It also gives you access to Pinterest's rich pins and other advanced features.

Optimizing your profile can increase your visibility. Use relevant keywords in your profile name, bio, and board descriptions. This will help your profile rank higher in search results and attract more followers. Make sure your profile reflects your brand and niche.

Creating engaging pins is crucial for attracting attention. Use high-quality images, clear text, and relevant keywords. Make your pins visually appealing and easy to understand. Include a clear call to action and a link to your affiliate product or landing page.

Utilizing keywords in pins can increase your reach. Conduct keyword research to find relevant and high-traffic keywords. Use these keywords in your pin titles, descriptions, and hashtags. This will help your pins rank higher in search results and attract more views.

Building your Pinterest boards can increase your engagement. Organize your pins into relevant boards and create a clear and concise board description. Use keywords and hashtags to increase the visibility of your boards. Make sure your boards are organized and easy to navigate.

Engaging with followers is important for building relationships. Respond to comments, repin relevant content, and participate in group boards. This will help you build a loyal following and increase your visibility. Engage with your followers regularly and provide valuable content.

Case studies of successful Pinterest marketers can provide valuable insights. Study what worked for others and apply similar tactics to your own efforts. This can help you achieve better results and avoid common mistakes. Learn from the best and adapt their strategies to your niche.

The role of Pinterest analytics is crucial for measuring success. Track key metrics like impressions, saves, and clicks. Use this data to understand how well your pins are performing and make informed decisions. Analyze your audience demographics and behavior to tailor your content accordingly.

Integrating affiliate links in pins can increase your sales. Include relevant links in your pin descriptions and provide context. This will help you promote your products without being too promotional. Encourage viewers to check out your links and provide honest reviews and recommendations.

Utilizing rich pins can enhance your pins. Rich pins provide additional information, such as product details, recipe ingredients, or article headlines. This can make your pins more informative and increase engagement. Enable rich pins on your website to take advantage of this feature.

Leveraging Pinterest ads can increase your reach. Use promoted pins to reach a larger audience and drive more traffic to your affiliate links. Experiment with different ad formats and targeting options to find what works best for you. Monitor your ad performance and adjust your campaigns as needed.

Best practices for Pinterest marketing include creating valuable content, optimizing for search, and engaging with your audience. Focus on providing value, being consistent, and continually improving your strategies. Experiment with different content formats, such as infographics, videos, and tutorials.

Avoiding common mistakes is important. Some common mistakes include being too promotional, neglecting SEO, and not engaging with your audience. Focus on creating valuable and engaging content, optimizing for search, and building relationships with your followers. Avoid spammy behavior and follow Pinterest's guidelines.

Creating pinnable images can increase your reach. Use high-quality images, clear text, and relevant keywords. Make your images visually appealing and easy to understand. Include a clear call to action and a link to your affiliate product or landing page.

Using group boards can increase your visibility. Join relevant group boards and share your content. This can help you reach a larger audience and increase your engagement. Follow the group board rules and engage with other members.

Staying consistent with pinning is essential. Create a content calendar and stick to a regular pinning schedule. This will help you maintain a steady flow of content and keep your audience engaged. Plan your content in advance and use scheduling tools to stay organized.

The importance of visual appeal cannot be overstated. Pinterest is a visual platform, and visually appealing pins are more likely to attract attention. Use high-quality images, clear text, and relevant keywords to make your pins stand out.

Engaging with Pinterest communities can increase your reach. Participate in relevant Pinterest groups, share your content, and engage with other members. This can help you build relationships and increase your visibility.

Leveraging trends and seasons can increase your reach. Create content that aligns with current trends and seasonal events. This can help you attract more views and stay relevant. Stay updated with the latest trends and adapt your content accordingly.

Building a Pinterest strategy can increase your effectiveness. Define your goals, create a content calendar, and track your progress. This will help you stay organized and achieve your marketing goals. Experiment with different strategies and continually improve your efforts.

Tools for Pinterest marketing can streamline your efforts. Use tools like Canva for designing pins, Tailwind for scheduling, and Pinterest Analytics for tracking performance. These tools can help you create high-quality content more efficiently. Experiment with different tools to find what works best for you.

Analyzing Pinterest metrics is important for measuring success. Track key metrics like impressions, saves, and clicks. Use this data to understand how well your pins are performing and make informed decisions. Analyze your audience demographics and behavior to tailor your content accordingly.

Staying updated with Pinterest trends is crucial. The Pinterest landscape is constantly evolving, and staying current with trends can help you stay ahead of the competition. Follow industry blogs, attend webinars, and participate in Pinterest communities to stay informed.

Future of Pinterest marketing looks promising. As more businesses invest in Pinterest marketing, new opportunities and trends will emerge. Stay adaptable and open to new strategies to stay ahead of the competition. Keep learning and experimenting with new content formats and techniques.

Chapter 10: Participating in Webinars and Online Workshops

Webinars and online workshops are valuable platforms for affiliate marketers. They allow you to engage with a targeted audience, share valuable information, and promote your affiliate products. Participating in these events can help you build relationships and increase your reach.

The basics of webinars include understanding the different types of webinars, choosing the right platform, and planning your content. Each platform has its own unique features and benefits. Choose the platforms that are most relevant to your niche and audience.

Choosing the right platform is crucial. Zoom, GoToWebinar, and Webex are popular options. Each platform has its own unique features and benefits. Choose the platforms that are most relevant to your niche and audience.

Planning your webinar content is important for engaging your audience. Focus on providing value, addressing your audience's needs, and promoting your affiliate products. Create a clear and concise outline and include relevant visuals and examples.

Engaging your audience is crucial for success. Use interactive elements, such as polls, Q&A sessions, and chat features, to keep your audience engaged. Respond to questions and encourage discussions to build relationships and increase engagement.

Utilizing affiliate links in webinars can increase your sales. Include relevant links in your webinar materials and provide context. This will help you promote your products without being too promotional. Encourage viewers to check out your links and provide honest reviews and recommendations.

Promoting your webinar is important for attracting attendees. Use social media, email marketing, and online communities to promote your event. Create eye-catching promotional materials and highlight the benefits of attending your webinar.

Case studies of successful webinars can provide valuable insights. Study what worked for others and apply similar tactics to your own events. This can help you achieve better results and avoid common mistakes. Learn from the best and adapt their strategies to your niche.

Avoiding common mistakes is important. Some common mistakes include being too promotional, neglecting to engage with the audience, and not providing valuable content. Focus on creating valuable and engaging webinars, optimizing for search, and building relationships with your attendees. Avoid spammy behavior and follow webinar guidelines.

Best practices for webinar presentations include being clear, concise, and engaging. Use relevant visuals, examples, and stories to illustrate your points. Practice your presentation in advance and be prepared to answer questions. Use a friendly and conversational tone to make your webinars more relatable.

The role of follow-up emails is crucial for maintaining engagement. Send follow-up emails to thank attendees, provide additional resources, and promote your affiliate products. This can help you build relationships and increase your chances of driving conversions.

Leveraging webinars for list building can increase your reach. Use webinars to attract new subscribers and build your email list. Offer valuable content, such as free ebooks, discounts, or access to exclusive content, to encourage sign-ups.

The importance of visuals cannot be overstated. Use high-quality images, videos, and graphics to make your webinars more engaging. Visuals can help illustrate your points, break up large blocks of text, and keep your audience's attention.

Integrating polls and Q&A sessions can increase engagement. Use polls to gather feedback, ask questions, and encourage discussions. This can help you engage your audience and make your webinars more interactive. Respond to questions and provide valuable insights.

Recording and repurposing webinars can extend their reach. Record your webinars and share the recordings on your website, social media, and email marketing campaigns. This can help you reach a larger audience and provide valuable content to those who couldn't attend live.

Building a webinar strategy can increase your effectiveness. Define your goals, create a content calendar, and track your progress. This will help you stay organized and achieve your marketing goals. Experiment with different strategies and continually improve your efforts.

The role of practice and preparation is important. Practice your presentation in advance and be prepared for technical issues. This will help you deliver a smooth and professional webinar. Prepare backup plans for technical difficulties and have a support team ready to assist.

Utilizing guest speakers can add value to your webinars. Invite experts and influencers in your niche to share their knowledge and insights. This can increase your credibility and attract more attendees. Collaborate with guest speakers to create engaging and informative content.

Engaging with attendees post-webinar can increase your reach. Follow up with attendees, answer their questions, and provide additional resources. This can help you build relationships and maintain engagement. Use follow-up emails, social media, and online communities to stay connected.

Analyzing webinar metrics is important for measuring success. Track key metrics like attendance, engagement, and conversions. Use this data to understand how well your webinars are performing and make informed decisions. Analyze your audience demographics and behavior to tailor your content accordingly.

Tools for webinar creation can streamline your efforts. Use tools like Zoom, GoToWebinar, and Canva for designing and managing your webinars. These tools can help you create high-quality webinars more efficiently. Experiment with different tools to find what works best for you.

The power of storytelling can make your webinars more engaging. Share personal anecdotes, case studies, and success stories. This will help you connect with your audience on an emotional level and make your content more relatable. Use storytelling to illustrate your points and provide valuable insights.

Staying consistent with webinars is essential. Create a content calendar and stick to a regular webinar schedule. This will help you maintain a steady flow of content and keep your audience engaged. Plan your content in advance and batch-produce webinars to stay ahead.

Integrating webinars with other marketing strategies can increase your overall effectiveness. Use webinars to complement your social media, email, and content marketing efforts. This can help you reach your audience through multiple touchpoints and increase your visibility.

Providing value to attendees is crucial for success. Focus on sharing valuable content, tips, and resources that are relevant to your niche. This can help you build a strong relationship with your audience and increase their willingness to follow your recommendations.

The future of webinar marketing looks promising. As more businesses invest in webinars, new opportunities and trends will emerge. Stay adaptable and open to new strategies to stay ahead of the competition. Keep learning and experimenting with new content formats and techniques.

Chapter 11: Engaging in Podcasting

———

Podcasting is a popular and effective way to share valuable content and promote your affiliate products. Podcasts allow you to reach a targeted audience, build a loyal following, and drive traffic to your affiliate links. Engaging in podcasting can help you achieve your marketing goals.

The rise of podcasting has been significant in recent years. Podcasts are convenient for your audience to consume and can cover a wide range of topics. By creating valuable and entertaining podcasts, you can attract a large audience and generate more sales.

Choosing a podcast niche is the first step. Focus on a specific area of interest or expertise that is relevant to your affiliate products. This will help you attract a targeted audience and create content that resonates with them. Conduct research to understand your audience's needs and preferences.

Planning your episodes is important for staying organized and consistent. Create a content calendar and outline your episodes in advance. This will help you maintain a steady flow of content and keep your audience engaged. Plan your content around relevant topics, trends, and events.

Recording high-quality audio is crucial for creating professional podcasts. Use a good microphone, soundproof your recording space, and minimize background noise. This will help you produce clear and crisp audio that is easy to listen to. Experiment with different recording setups to find what works best for you.

Editing your podcasts is important for creating polished and professional episodes. Use editing software to trim, add effects, and enhance your audio. Make sure your podcasts are well-produced and free of errors. Experiment with different editing styles to find what works best for your audience.

Promoting your podcast is crucial for attracting listeners. Use social media, email marketing, and online communities to promote your episodes. Create eye-catching promotional materials and highlight the benefits of listening to your podcast. Encourage your audience to subscribe, leave reviews, and share your episodes.

Utilizing affiliate links in podcasts can increase your sales. Include relevant links in your podcast show notes and provide context. This will help you promote your products without being too promotional. Encourage listeners to check out your links and provide honest reviews and recommendations.

Case studies of successful podcasts can provide valuable insights. Study what worked for others and apply similar tactics to your own podcast. This can help you achieve better results and avoid common mistakes. Learn from the best and adapt their strategies to your niche.

Avoiding common mistakes is important. Some common mistakes include being too promotional, neglecting to engage with the audience, and not providing valuable content. Focus on creating valuable and engaging podcasts, optimizing for search, and building relationships with your listeners. Avoid spammy behavior and follow podcasting guidelines.

Best practices for podcasting include being clear, concise, and engaging. Use relevant examples, stories, and interviews to illustrate your points. Practice your delivery and be prepared to answer questions. Use a friendly and conversational tone to make your podcasts more relatable.

Engaging with your audience is crucial for building relationships. Respond to listener feedback, ask questions, and encourage discussions. This will help you build a loyal following and increase engagement. Create a community around your podcast and foster a sense of belonging.

The role of guest interviews is important for adding value to your podcasts. Invite experts and influencers in your niche to share their knowledge and insights. This can increase your credibility and attract more listeners. Collaborate with guest speakers to create engaging and informative content.

Monetizing your podcast can be done in various ways. Use affiliate links, sponsored content, or ads to generate revenue. Experiment with different monetization strategies to find what works best for you. Apply for podcast sponsorships and partnerships to earn money from your episodes.

Building a podcast strategy can increase your effectiveness. Define your goals, create a content calendar, and track your progress. This will help you stay organized and achieve your marketing goals. Experiment with different strategies and continually improve your efforts.

Utilizing podcast directories can increase your reach. Submit your podcast to popular directories like Apple Podcasts, Spotify, and Google Podcasts. This will help you reach a larger audience and increase your visibility. Optimize your podcast metadata with relevant keywords and descriptions.

Creating show notes can enhance your podcast episodes. Include a summary of the episode, key points, and relevant links. This will provide additional value to your listeners and help them find the information they need. Use clear and concise language to make your show notes easy to read.

Leveraging social media for promotion can increase your reach. Share your podcast episodes on your social media profiles, join relevant groups, and engage with your audience. This can help you attract more listeners and drive more traffic to your episodes. Use relevant hashtags and tags to increase visibility.

Analyzing podcast metrics is important for measuring success. Track key metrics like downloads, listens, and engagement. Use this data to understand how well your podcasts are performing and make informed decisions. Analyze your audience demographics and behavior to tailor your content accordingly.

Staying consistent with episodes is essential. Create a content calendar and stick to a regular posting schedule. This will help you maintain a steady flow of content and keep your audience engaged. Plan your content in advance and batch-produce episodes to stay ahead.

The power of storytelling can make your podcasts more engaging. Share personal anecdotes, case studies, and success stories. This will help you connect with your audience on an emotional level and make your content more relatable. Use storytelling to illustrate your points and provide valuable insights.

Engaging with listeners is crucial for building relationships. Respond to listener feedback, ask questions, and encourage discussions. This will help you build a loyal following and increase engagement. Create a community around your podcast and foster a sense of belonging.

Tools for podcasting can streamline your efforts. Use tools like Audacity for editing, Buzzsprout for hosting, and Canva for designing promotional materials. These tools can help you create high-quality podcasts more efficiently. Experiment with different tools to find what works best for you.

Integrating podcasts with other marketing strategies can increase your overall effectiveness. Use podcasts to complement your social media, email, and content marketing efforts. This can help you reach your audience through multiple touchpoints and increase your visibility.

Providing value to listeners is crucial for success. Focus on sharing valuable content, tips, and resources that are relevant to your niche. This can help you build a strong relationship with your audience and increase their willingness to follow your recommendations.

The future of podcast marketing looks promising. As more businesses invest in podcasts, new opportunities and trends will emerge. Stay adaptable and open to new strategies to stay ahead of the competition. Keep learning and experimenting with new content formats and techniques.

Chapter 12: Participating in Affiliate Networks

Affiliate networks are platforms that connect affiliates with merchants. They provide a central place for affiliates to find and promote products, track their performance, and receive payments. Participating in affiliate networks can help you find high-quality products and increase your affiliate marketing success.

Understanding affiliate networks is the first step. Affiliate networks act as intermediaries between affiliates and merchants. They provide a platform for affiliates to find and promote products, track their performance, and receive payments. Some popular affiliate networks include Amazon Associates, ShareASale, and ClickBank.

Choosing the right network is crucial. Each network has its own unique features, benefits, and product offerings. Choose the networks that are most relevant to your niche and audience. Conduct research to understand the commission rates, payment terms, and product quality of each network.

Setting up your account is important for getting started. Create an account on the chosen affiliate network, complete your profile, and provide the necessary information. This will help you access the network's features and start promoting products.

Finding the best offers is crucial for maximizing your earnings. Use the network's search and filtering tools to find high-quality products that are relevant to your niche. Look for products with high commission rates, positive reviews, and good sales performance.

Analyzing offer metrics can help you make informed decisions. Look at key metrics like conversion rates, average order value, and earnings per click. Use this data to understand the performance of different offers and choose the best ones to promote.

Building relationships with affiliate managers can provide valuable support. Affiliate managers can help you find the best offers, provide promotional materials, and offer advice on improving your performance. Engage with them regularly and seek their guidance to maximize your success.

Case studies of successful affiliates can provide valuable insights. Study what worked for others and apply similar tactics to your own efforts. This can help you achieve better results and avoid common mistakes. Learn from the best and adapt their strategies to your niche.

Avoiding common mistakes is important. Some common mistakes include promoting low-quality products, not tracking your performance, and not engaging with your audience. Focus on promoting high-quality products, tracking your results, and building relationships with your audience.

Best practices for network engagement include being active, providing value, and following the network's guidelines. Engage with the network's community, share your knowledge, and provide helpful insights. This will help you build credibility and trust with other affiliates and merchants.

Utilizing network tools and resources can streamline your efforts. Most affiliate networks provide tools for tracking performance, creating promotional materials, and managing your account. Use these tools to optimize your efforts and achieve better results.

Integrating offers with your marketing strategies can increase your sales. Use a mix of social media, email marketing, content marketing, and paid advertising to promote your affiliate offers. This can help you reach a larger audience and drive more traffic to your affiliate links.

The role of tracking and analytics is crucial for measuring success. Use the network's tracking tools to monitor your clicks, conversions, and earnings. Analyze this data to understand how well your efforts are performing and make informed decisions.

Staying updated with network trends is important. The affiliate marketing landscape is constantly evolving, and staying current with trends can help you stay ahead of the competition. Follow industry blogs, attend webinars, and participate in network communities to stay informed.

Leveraging network promotions can increase your earnings. Many networks offer promotions, bonuses, and incentives to boost your performance. Take advantage of these opportunities to maximize your earnings and achieve your goals.

Engaging with other affiliates can provide valuable insights. Participate in network forums, join affiliate communities, and share your experiences. This can help you learn from others, build relationships, and stay motivated.

Utilizing network forums and communities can increase your visibility. Participate in relevant discussions, share valuable content, and provide helpful insights. This will help you build a positive reputation and attract more attention to your affiliate offers.

The importance of compliance cannot be overstated. Ensure that your promotional efforts comply with the network's guidelines and advertising regulations. This will help you avoid legal issues and maintain a positive reputation.

Building long-term relationships with networks can increase your success. Focus on providing value, maintaining open communication, and being respectful of their time and efforts. This will help you build strong, lasting partnerships.

Maximizing your earnings requires a strategic approach. Choose high-quality offers, optimize your promotional efforts, and continually improve your strategies. Use a mix of marketing channels and track your performance to achieve better results.

Utilizing network training resources can enhance your skills. Many affiliate networks offer training materials, webinars, and courses to help you improve your performance. Take advantage of these resources to learn new strategies and stay updated with industry trends.

Integrating multiple networks can increase your reach. Join several affiliate networks to access a wider range of products and opportunities. This can help you diversify your income and reduce your reliance on a single network.

Tools for affiliate network engagement can streamline your efforts. Use tools like Google Analytics for tracking, Canva for creating promotional materials, and Hootsuite for managing social media. These tools can help you optimize your efforts and achieve better results.

Analyzing network performance is important for measuring success. Track key metrics like clicks, conversions, and earnings. Use this data to understand how well your efforts are performing and make informed decisions. Analyze your performance regularly and adjust your strategies accordingly.

Providing feedback to networks can improve your experience. Share your experiences, suggestions, and concerns with the network's support team. This can help you build a positive relationship and improve the network's features and services.

Future of affiliate networks looks promising. As more businesses invest in affiliate marketing, new opportunities and trends will emerge. Stay adaptable and open to new strategies to stay ahead of the competition. Keep learning and experimenting with new offers and techniques.

Chapter 13: Leveraging Ebooks and Online Courses

Ebooks and online courses are valuable content formats that can help you promote your affiliate products. They allow you to share in-depth information, attract a targeted audience, and drive traffic to your affiliate links. Leveraging these formats can help you achieve your marketing goals.

The basics of creating ebooks include choosing the right topic, writing engaging content, and designing your ebook. Choose a topic that is relevant to your niche and provides value to your audience. Conduct research to gather information and insights, and write clear and concise content that addresses your audience's needs.

Choosing the right topic is crucial for attracting readers. Focus on a specific area of interest or expertise that is relevant to your affiliate products. This will help you attract a targeted audience and create content that resonates with them. Conduct research to understand your audience's needs and preferences.

Writing engaging content is important for keeping your readers interested. Use a friendly and conversational tone, provide valuable information, and include relevant examples and stories. Break up large blocks of text with headings, bullet points, and images to make your ebook more readable.

Designing your ebook can make it more visually appealing. Use high-quality images, clear text, and a professional layout. Make sure your ebook reflects your brand and is easy to navigate. Use tools like Canva or Adobe InDesign to create a polished and professional design.

Promoting your ebook is crucial for attracting readers. Use social media, email marketing, and online communities to promote your ebook. Create eye-catching promotional materials and highlight the benefits of reading your ebook. Encourage your audience to download, read, and share your ebook.

Utilizing affiliate links in ebooks can increase your sales. Include relevant links in your ebook and provide context. This will help you promote your products without being too promotional. Encourage readers to check out your links and provide honest reviews and recommendations.

Case studies of successful ebooks can provide valuable insights. Study what worked for others and apply similar tactics to your own ebook. This can help you achieve better results and avoid common mistakes. Learn from the best and adapt their strategies to your niche.

Avoiding common mistakes is important. Some common mistakes include being too promotional, neglecting to provide value, and not engaging with your audience. Focus on creating valuable and engaging ebooks, optimizing for search, and building relationships with your readers. Avoid spammy behavior and follow ebook guidelines.

Best practices for ebook marketing include being clear, concise, and engaging. Use relevant examples, stories, and case studies to illustrate your points. Practice your delivery and be prepared to answer questions. Use a friendly and conversational tone to make your ebooks more relatable.

Creating online courses can increase your reach and credibility. Online courses allow you to share in-depth knowledge and provide value to your audience. Choose a topic that is relevant to your niche and create a structured and comprehensive course. Use a mix of video, text, and interactive elements to engage your audience.

Choosing the right platform is crucial for hosting your course. Udemy, Teachable, and Thinkific are popular options. Each platform has its own unique features and benefits. Choose the platforms that are most relevant to your niche and audience.

Planning your course content is important for staying organized and consistent. Create a content calendar and outline your course in advance. This will help you maintain a steady flow of content and keep your audience engaged. Plan your content around relevant topics, trends, and events.

Recording high-quality videos is crucial for creating professional courses. Use a good microphone, soundproof your recording space, and minimize background noise. This will help you produce clear and crisp audio that is easy to listen to. Experiment with different recording setups to find what works best for you.

Engaging with course participants is crucial for building relationships. Respond to questions, provide feedback, and encourage discussions. This will help you build a loyal following and increase engagement. Create a community around your course and foster a sense of belonging.

Utilizing affiliate links in courses can increase your sales. Include relevant links in your course materials and provide context. This will help you promote your products without being too promotional. Encourage participants to check out your links and provide honest reviews and recommendations.

Promoting your course is important for attracting participants. Use social media, email marketing, and online communities to promote your course. Create eye-catching promotional materials and highlight the benefits of taking your course. Encourage your audience to enroll, participate, and share your course.

Analyzing course performance is important for measuring success. Track key metrics like enrollments, engagement, and conversions. Use this data to understand how well your courses are performing and make informed decisions. Analyze your audience demographics and behavior to tailor your content accordingly.

Leveraging student testimonials can increase your credibility. Encourage students to share their experiences and provide feedback. Use their testimonials in your promotional materials to attract more participants. Highlight the success stories and positive outcomes from your course.

Integrating courses with other marketing strategies can increase your overall effectiveness. Use courses to complement your social media, email, and content marketing efforts. This can help you reach your audience through multiple touchpoints and increase your visibility.

Providing value to students is crucial for success. Focus on sharing valuable content, tips, and resources that are relevant to your niche. This can help you build a strong relationship with your audience and increase their willingness to follow your recommendations.

The future of online education looks promising. As more businesses invest in online courses, new opportunities and trends will emerge. Stay adaptable and open to new strategies to stay ahead of the competition. Keep learning and experimenting with new content formats and techniques.

Chapter 14: Utilizing Local Marketing Strategies

Local marketing strategies can be effective for promoting your affiliate products within your community. By engaging with local businesses, events, and groups, you can build relationships and increase your reach. Utilizing these strategies can help you achieve your marketing goals.

The importance of local marketing cannot be overstated. Local marketing allows you to connect with people in your community, build trust, and promote your products. Focus on providing value and building relationships to achieve success.

Building relationships with local businesses can increase your reach. Partner with local businesses to promote your affiliate products. This can include co-hosting events, offering exclusive discounts, or creating joint promotions. Build strong relationships and provide value to your partners.

Utilizing local events and meetups can increase your visibility. Participate in local events, meetups, and networking groups. This can help you connect with potential customers and build relationships. Share your knowledge, provide value, and promote your affiliate products.

Creating local content can attract a targeted audience. Write blog posts, create videos, and share social media content that is relevant to your local community. Highlight local events, businesses, and issues to engage your audience and build trust.

Engaging with your local community is crucial for building relationships. Participate in local forums, join community groups, and engage with local influencers. This will help you build a loyal following and increase your visibility.

Utilizing local social media groups can increase your reach. Join relevant local groups on Facebook, LinkedIn, and other social media platforms. Share valuable content, participate in discussions, and promote your affiliate products. Engage with group members regularly to build relationships.

Case studies of successful local marketing can provide valuable insights. Study what worked for others and apply similar tactics to your own efforts. This can help you achieve better results and avoid common mistakes. Learn from the best and adapt their strategies to your community.

Avoiding common mistakes is important. Some common mistakes include being too promotional, neglecting to provide value, and not engaging with your community. Focus on creating valuable and engaging content, optimizing for search, and building relationships with your audience. Avoid spammy behavior and follow local marketing guidelines.

Best practices for local marketing include being clear, concise, and engaging. Use relevant examples, stories, and case studies to illustrate your points. Practice your delivery and be prepared to answer questions. Use a friendly and conversational tone to make your local marketing efforts more relatable.

Integrating local marketing with affiliate links can increase your sales. Include relevant links in your local content and provide context. This will help you promote your products without being too promotional. Encourage your audience to check out your links and provide honest reviews and recommendations.

Leveraging local influencers can increase your reach. Partner with local influencers to promote your affiliate products. This can include co-hosting events, creating joint content, and offering exclusive discounts. Build strong relationships and provide value to your partners.

The role of local SEO is crucial for increasing your visibility. Optimize your website and online profiles with relevant local keywords. This will help you rank higher in local search results and attract more traffic. Use tools like Google My Business to manage your local listings and improve your visibility.

Building a local marketing strategy can increase your effectiveness. Define your goals, create a content calendar, and track your progress. This will help you stay organized and achieve your marketing goals. Experiment with different strategies and continually improve your efforts.

Engaging with local media can increase your visibility. Reach out to local newspapers, magazines, and radio stations to share your story. This can help you attract more attention and build credibility. Create press releases, pitch your story, and provide valuable insights to local media outlets.

Utilizing local advertising can increase your reach. Use local newspapers, magazines, and online platforms to promote your affiliate products. Experiment with different ad formats and targeting options to find what works best for you. Monitor your ad performance and adjust your campaigns as needed.

Analyzing local marketing metrics is important for measuring success. Track key metrics like traffic, engagement, and conversions. Use this data to understand how well your local marketing efforts are performing and make informed decisions. Analyze your audience demographics and behavior to tailor your content accordingly.

Staying updated with local trends is important. The local marketing landscape is constantly evolving, and staying current with trends can help you stay ahead of the competition. Follow industry blogs, attend local events, and participate in community discussions to stay informed.

The importance of networking cannot be overstated. Build relationships with local business owners, influencers, and community leaders. This can help you increase your reach, build credibility, and achieve your marketing goals. Participate in local events, join networking groups, and engage with your community regularly.

Providing value to your local community is crucial for success. Focus on sharing valuable content, tips, and resources that are relevant to your audience. This can help you build a strong relationship with your community and increase their willingness to follow your recommendations.

Leveraging local partnerships can increase your reach. Partner with local businesses, organizations, and influencers to promote your affiliate products.

This can include co-hosting events, creating joint content, and offering exclusive discounts. Build strong relationships and provide value to your partners.

Creating local workshops and seminars can increase your visibility. Host workshops and seminars focused on your niche and provide valuable information to your audience. This can help you build relationships, showcase your expertise, and promote your affiliate products.

Utilizing local email marketing can increase your engagement. Build an email list of local subscribers and send regular newsletters with valuable content, tips, and promotions. This can help you stay connected with your audience and drive more traffic to your affiliate links.

Building a local personal brand can increase your credibility. Establish yourself as an authority in your niche and build trust with your community. Share your knowledge, provide value, and engage with your audience regularly. This will help you attract more attention and increase your chances of success.

Tools for local marketing can streamline your efforts. Use tools like Google My Business for managing local listings, Canva for creating promotional materials, and Hootsuite for managing social media. These tools can help you optimize your efforts and achieve better results.

Future of local marketing looks promising. As more businesses invest in local marketing, new opportunities and trends will emerge. Stay adaptable and open to new strategies to stay ahead of the competition. Keep learning and experimenting with new content formats and techniques.

Chapter 15: Building Long-Term Relationships with Your Audience

———

Building long-term relationships with your audience is crucial for affiliate marketing success. By engaging with your audience, providing consistent value, and building trust, you can create a loyal following and increase your sales. Focus on building relationships to achieve your marketing goals.

The importance of relationship building cannot be overstated. Building strong relationships with your audience can increase their trust and loyalty. Focus on providing value, engaging with your audience, and building trust to achieve success.

Engaging with your audience is crucial for building relationships. Respond to comments, ask questions, and encourage discussions. This will help you build a loyal following and increase engagement. Create a community around your brand and foster a sense of belonging.

Providing consistent value is important for maintaining engagement. Share valuable content, tips, and resources that are relevant to your audience. This can help you build a strong relationship with your audience and increase their willingness to follow your recommendations.

Building trust and credibility is crucial for success. Be honest, transparent, and reliable in your communications. This will help you build trust with your audience and increase their willingness to follow your recommendations.

Utilizing social proof can increase trust and credibility. Share testimonials, reviews, and case studies to build trust with your audience. This will help you attract more attention and increase your chances of success.

Responding to feedback is important for building relationships. Listen to your audience's feedback, address their concerns, and make improvements based on their suggestions. This will help you build a stronger relationship with your audience and increase their satisfaction.

Case studies of successful relationship building can provide valuable insights. Study what worked for others and apply similar tactics to your own efforts. This can help you achieve better results and avoid common mistakes. Learn from the best and adapt their strategies to your niche.

Avoiding common mistakes is important. Some common mistakes include being too promotional, neglecting to engage with your audience, and not providing value. Focus on building relationships, providing value, and maintaining a positive reputation.

Best practices for audience engagement include being responsive, providing value, and following the community guidelines. Engage with your audience regularly, share valuable content, and provide helpful insights. This will help you build credibility and trust with your audience.

Utilizing multiple communication channels can increase your reach. Use a mix of social media, email marketing, content marketing, and online communities to engage with your audience. This can help you reach a larger audience and increase your visibility.

The role of personalization is important for building relationships. Personalize your communications to make them more relevant and relatable. Use your audience's names, include personalized recommendations, and tailor your content to their interests and preferences.

Integrating relationship building with affiliate marketing can increase your sales. Focus on building relationships with your audience and providing value. This will help you build trust and increase their willingness to follow your recommendations.

Staying consistent with communication is crucial for maintaining engagement. Create a content calendar and stick to a regular posting schedule. This will help you maintain a steady flow of content and keep your audience engaged. Plan your content in advance and use scheduling tools to stay organized.

Leveraging user-generated content can increase trust and credibility. Encourage your audience to share their experiences and contribute content. Share their content on your own platforms to show appreciation and build a sense of community.

Building a community around your brand can increase loyalty and engagement. Encourage your followers to participate in discussions, share their experiences, and connect with each other. This will help you create a supportive and engaged community.

Engaging with your audience offline can increase your reach. Participate in local events, host workshops, and meetups to engage with your audience in person. This can help you build stronger relationships and increase your visibility.

Utilizing surveys and polls can provide valuable insights. Use surveys and polls to gather feedback, understand your audience's needs, and tailor your content accordingly. This will help you provide more relevant and valuable content to your audience.

Analyzing audience engagement metrics is important for measuring success. Track key metrics like engagement, reach, and conversions. Use this data to understand how well your efforts are performing and make informed decisions. Analyze your audience demographics and behavior to tailor your content accordingly.

Staying updated with audience trends is crucial. The audience landscape is constantly evolving, and staying current with trends can help you stay ahead of the competition. Follow industry blogs, attend webinars, and participate in community discussions to stay informed.

The importance of authenticity cannot be overstated. Be genuine, transparent, and relatable in your communications. This will help you build trust with your audience and increase their willingness to follow your recommendations.

Providing exceptional customer service can increase trust and loyalty. Respond to customer inquiries promptly, address their concerns, and go above and beyond to meet their needs. This will help you build a strong relationship with your audience and increase their satisfaction.

Building long-term loyalty is crucial for success. Focus on providing consistent value, engaging with your audience, and building trust. This will help you create a loyal following and increase your chances of long-term success.

Leveraging testimonials and reviews can increase trust and credibility. Encourage your audience to share their experiences and provide feedback. Use their testimonials in your promotional materials to attract more attention and build trust.

Tools for relationship building can streamline your efforts. Use tools like Hootsuite for managing social media, Mailchimp for email marketing, and Google Analytics for tracking performance. These tools can help you optimize your efforts and achieve better results.

Future of audience engagement looks promising. As more businesses invest in relationship building, new opportunities and trends will emerge. Stay adaptable and open to new strategies to stay ahead of the competition. Keep learning and experimenting with new content formats and techniques.

Your Journey Ahead

Recapping the key points, it's clear that affiliate marketing without a website is not only possible but also highly effective. By leveraging various platforms and strategies, you can build a successful affiliate marketing business. Remember to stay patient, consistent, and willing to learn.

Your journey in affiliate marketing is just beginning. Embrace the challenges and opportunities that come your way. Stay updated with industry trends and continually improve your strategies. The path to success is paved with persistence, dedication, and continuous learning.

As you move forward, focus on building strong relationships with your audience. Provide consistent value, engage with your followers, and build trust. This will help you create a loyal following and increase your chances of long-term success.

Innovation and creativity are key to staying ahead in the affiliate marketing landscape. Experiment with new strategies, content formats, and platforms. Don't be afraid to take risks and think outside the box.

Your skills and knowledge are your greatest assets. Continue to hone your skills, learn new techniques, and stay updated with industry trends. This will help you stay competitive and achieve your marketing goals.

Engaging with the affiliate marketing community can provide valuable support. Join online forums, attend webinars, and participate in community discussions. This will help you learn from others, share your experiences, and stay motivated.

As you build your affiliate marketing business, remember the importance of providing value. Focus on creating content that meets the needs of your audience and provides valuable insights. This will help you build a strong relationship with your audience and increase their willingness to follow your recommendations.

Setting future goals is crucial for staying focused and motivated. Define what you want to achieve and create a plan to get there. Break down your goals into smaller, manageable tasks and track your progress along the way.

The power of networking cannot be overstated. Build relationships with other affiliates, influencers, and industry experts. This can help you increase your reach, build credibility, and achieve your marketing goals.

Engaging with mentors and coaches can provide valuable guidance. Seek out experienced affiliates and industry experts who can offer advice and support. This can help you navigate challenges and achieve your goals more effectively.

Building a personal brand can increase your credibility and reach. Establish yourself as an authority in your niche and build trust with your audience. Share your knowledge, provide value, and engage with your audience regularly.

Integrating multiple marketing strategies can increase your overall effectiveness. Use a mix of social media, email marketing, content marketing, and paid advertising to reach your audience. This can help you create a comprehensive marketing plan and achieve better results.

Adaptability is crucial for success in affiliate marketing. The landscape is constantly evolving, and staying adaptable can help you stay ahead of the competition. Embrace change, learn new strategies, and be open to new opportunities.

Building a legacy in affiliate marketing is about more than just making money. Focus on providing value, building relationships, and making a positive impact. This will help you create a lasting legacy and achieve long-term success.

Providing value to the next generation of affiliate marketers is important. Share your knowledge, mentor new affiliates, and contribute to the community. This can help you build a positive reputation and make a lasting impact.

Staying true to your vision is crucial for achieving your goals. Define your vision, create a plan, and stay focused. This will help you stay motivated and achieve your marketing goals.

Embracing change and growth is essential for success. The affiliate marketing landscape is constantly evolving, and staying open to change can help you stay ahead of the competition. Embrace new opportunities, learn new skills, and continuously improve your strategies.

Building a community of support can increase your chances of success. Surround yourself with like-minded individuals who can offer advice, support, and motivation. This can help you stay focused, motivated, and achieve your goals more effectively.

Your path to long-term success in affiliate marketing is paved with persistence, dedication, and continuous learning. Stay focused, stay motivated, and keep learning. With time and effort, you can achieve your marketing goals and build a successful affiliate marketing business without a website.

www.ingramcontent.com/pod-product-compliance
Lightning Source LLC
Chambersburg PA
CBHW030035230526
45472CB00002B/514